The Psychology of Religion

Joseph McCabe

Contents

I. Our Age of Psychology
II. The Religion of Woman
III. Religion and Psycho-Analysis
IV. The Religious Instinct
V. The Herd-Instinct and Religion
VI. The Psychology of the Fanatic

Chapter I

Our Age Of Psychology

Some years ago I wrote a work, *The Evolution of Mind,* in which I used almost the entire teaching of four or five branches of science to throw light on one single issue: whether mind is a function of the nervous system and how, as such, it came into being. I then held the eccentric opinion that the first object of any science was to tell us the nature of the reality or realities it studied; that the first question which thoughtful people would put to a science of mind is, in view of the world-wide interest in the subject, whether the mind is a spiritual intruder in a material universe or merely a function of the steadily developing nervous system. And the only men who failed to appreciate my work were the psychologists. "That," said a St. Louis professor, fraternally but firmly, to me, "is not psychology."

The evolution of psychology is a proof that science has not yet completely emancipated itself from its serfdom to religious beliefs. It was originally a branch of philosophy, and its chief purpose was to serve religion by furnishing convincing proofs that the soul is spiritual and immortal. In proportion as the methods of science were adopted in it, and arguments of a philosophical character were eliminated, the aim of the science was changed. Half a century ago it abandoned the word "soul," and it threw out the question of immortality as a minor irrelevance to be wrangled over by Materialists, Christians, Spiritualists, and Theosophists.

Then psychology ceased to concern itself about the nature of the mind or consciousness, and declared that its aim was to study states of consciousness. How there could be "states" of something without something of which they were states was left to philosophers, but thirty or forty years ago the common phrase was that all that we had to study was a stream of states of consciousness. Now, in the current joke, psychology has even "lost consciousness," and the unfortunate person who wants really to know what mind is -- a question the answer to which is supposed to affect the very foundation of human life -- finds no guidance or assistance in any branch of science or even in modern philosophy.

And thus there came about the paradox of modern psychology, that it spreads itself over a field of vast extent and steadily refuses to consider the chief question that occurs to the mind about itself. We have a psychology of everything, from education to salesmanship, from the heroine of the novel or the film to the art of advertising, from the baby to the bishop, from the criminal to the saint. In another ten years we shall have psychologies of wallpapers, soft drinks (I have heard an expert divide humanity into white coffee and black coffee people), toothbrushes, cigarettes, neckwear, and griddle cakes. About a million people in America make a good living out of the other hundred and fifteen millions by psychologizing about them. The store, the studio, and the school reek with psychology. It explains everything, from the commission and detection of crime to the baby's love of mud and its grandpa's weakness for erotic films.

How much more we know about human nature than Abraham Lincoln or Oliver Wendell Holmes did I am not quite sure, but, setting aside all the humorous exaggerations and commercial exploitations of the word, the ideal is excellent. We are to apply scientific method -- which in the long run means merely more careful observation -- to every form of human behavior. The only groan of the pessimist that is worth a moment's consideration is his plea that our conduct is no wiser or better than that of the Athenians of two thousand years ago or of the Egyptians and Babylonians of four thousand years ago. Let us, by all means, give the stars and electrons and buried fossils a spell of rest, and turn this very wonderful apparatus of science upon life. Let us have a quite candid, scientific analysis of the behavior of pivotal people like the politician and his agent, the policeman, the preacher, the storekeeper (as well as the customer), the reformer, and so on.

Anyhow, since the religious part of man's behavior is said to be the most important and most interesting of all, it ought to be the first to attract the psychologic eye. Here, however, the shadow of the great prohibitionist Moses lies across the path, and the psychologist either turns away or becomes remarkably timid and accommodating. We have had a score of works on the psychology -- of religion in the last twenty years, and they are all bad. You may take the most sagacious writer of them all, William James (*Varieties of Religious Experience*), and if you care to make a real study of any one of the religious characters that he reviews -- say St. Augustine -- you will realize that his "Psychology" is a very different thing from accurate biography. Other professors write thousands of pages on the subject, carefully premising that what they say must not be regarded as a criticism of the *value* of religion, but you do not feel much clearer in the end as to why your neighbor holds religious views, or why your wife or daughter should be distressed to the marrow of her dear little soul because you won't go to church.

The best recent book on the subject, and a comparatively small book, is *An Introduction to the Psychology of Religion* (1923) by R. H. Thouless, lecturer on psychology in a British university. He hits the nail on the head. Unfortunately, he also hammers the boards a good deal in the usual style, but he does give a sensible analysis of ordinary religious belief. He correctly says that the task is to "express the workings of the mind when it is religious in terms of the mental processes we have discovered in secular psychology." He avoids the question of the origin of religion, which really, though it fascinates the professors as a rule, throws little or no light on religious belief today. We wore clothes originally to keep ourselves warm: we now wear them to keep other people cold. And Mr. Thouless will have none of these fantastic theories which "create a new and mystifying psychology for religion alone." We form religious beliefs, and have corresponding emotions, as we form political beliefs.

And here we find in this in many ways excellent book the same defect as in all the others. They almost entirely ignore -- generally do ignore entirely -- the most important element of all: priestcraft, by which I mean here simply the trade of the priest. He is no villain because he wants people to appreciate his wares, but the fact is that if he did not push them in the way he does, all the other "psychological" factors would amount to very little. Interest in politics would be feeble if there were no political orators, although political conduct is certainly concerned with grave realities of life. How much real interest in religion would there be if a hundred thousand clergymen did not make it their proper and very earnest business to keep that interest alive?

Most people have only to reflect, say, on all the people in their own block to realize this, but I will give here one historical illustration. The American population is especially composed of religious, and often fanatical, contingents from nations of the old world who had suffered persecution; and even in the last hundred years the main streams of immigration (Irish, Italian, Polish, Jewish, etc.) have predominantly brought religious fanatics, because they naturally came from the poorest, least educated, and most overcrowded countries, which means the most religious.

Now consider the fortunes of the most fanatical of them all, the Roman Catholics, when the great expansion of the American people toward the Pacific took place in the nineteenth century. It is true that there were not priests enough to found chapels wherever a few hundred Catholics settled -- a difficulty which Rome can always overcome by consecrating German or Belgian peasants and drafting them abroad -- but the main point was that priests were generally disinclined to leave Boston and Philadelphia and rough it with the western pioneers. The result was that in a few decades literally millions of these fanatical Catholics lost all interest in religion. In 1836 Bishop England (Catholic bishop of Charlestown) was requested by Rome to draw up, in Rome, a careful statement of the facts. He estimated that between 1815 and 1836 the Church had lost 3,750,000 people. It was worse afterwards during the western expansion and the big Irish, Italian, and Polish invasions. I may deal with the matter in a later Little Blue Book, and will say here only that in 1891 a group of American Catholics addressed a memorial (the Lucerne Memorial) to the Pope bewailing that 16,000,000 had apostatized. The *Vérité* of Quebec made the same estimate, independently, in 1898. The New York *Freeman's Journal* in the same year put the loss at twenty millions, and I have shown from immigration analyses that the loss was at least fourteen or fifteen millions.

In other words, the most fanatical of all religious adherents fell away in masses when there were no priests to bother them, and, although priests came along as soon as there was money enough in any town to give a middle-class income to an ordained peasant, they never recovered the apostates or (in most cases) their children. I could fill a large volume with these concrete and overwhelming illustrations of the supreme importance of the priest or minister, yet he is scarcely ever mentioned In discussions of the psychology of religion. It would be "superficial" to explain religious belief in that way.... Anyhow, it would not be prudent.

You do not look for prudence, but plain English, in Haldeman-Julius publications, and we shall see here what amount of truth there is in the various psychologies of religion. We are going, together, to examine the religious beliefs of the men and women you actually know. Academic writers are very apt to construct their own "religious man," and too often they construct him to fit a preconceived theory of what he ought to be. Other writers take eccentric and exceptional types of believers and make general theories of religion out of their analysis of these. Let us try, as far as possible, to ascertain the actual attitudes of a very great variety of religious men and women -- there is, of course, no such thing as *a* religious type -- and see what influences give them the different shades of religious belief or emotion which most of us lack.

Chapter II

The Religion of Woman

And the first popular fallacy about the psychology of religion which we have to expose is the idea that women are in a very large proportion more religious than men. Here even the reader who finds me generally cautious about my facts and reasonable about my deductions will begin to protest. Surely, he will say, it is notorious in every land, has been notorious in all ages and literature, that woman is more religious than man. The clergy themselves almost universally believe it, and they ought to know.

Let me remind you that a great many things which are not true have been believed in all countries and ages, and many of these beliefs relate to woman. It has been universally believed that woman is more sensitive than man, yet it has been proved repeatedly in the psychological laboratories of America that she is not. It has been held widely in all literatures, and is widely held today, that a woman knows things by "intuition," and one need know little psychology to see that this is a miserable fallacy: that the "intuition" (which exists more abundantly in fiction than in life) is simply a hasty deduction, unconscious of its own premises. When I worked in the Feminist movement, ten to twenty years ago, I found it the quite general and dogmatic belief of my lady friends that woman is innately, or on principle more virtuous than man; and it was to them quite a new, though obvious, idea when I pointed out that if, in sexual intercourse, the *male* ran the risk of pregnancy, all the coyness and virtue would be on *his* side, and that familiarity with the use of preventives is already altering this distribution of virtue.

But let fact precede argument. In the last chapter I gave from American experience a set of facts which abundantly prove my thesis, that the chief influence in religious belief is the activity of the priest. Now let me give a set of facts from British life which are worth more than a volume of argument or psychology about the religion of woman.

In the years 1902-1903 there was an accurate and scientific enumeration of the people who go to church in the city of London. There had been a similar, though less systematic, enumeration in 1886, and religious people, encouraged by the optimistic assurances of their clergy, desired a fresh enumeration, which should make an end of this wicked cry that religion was in decay. An important metropolitan journal, under religious control, organized the census. It was spread over a year, so as to give a balance of good and bad weather, and it was conducted by religious, but broad-minded men. Every man, woman, and child of the six million people of London who went to church during that period was individually counted, and a liberal estimate of "twicers" (people who went twice on one Sunday) was deducted so as to give, approximately, the actual number of people who go to church more or less regularly in the largest city of the world.

To the general lessons of this census I return in another Little Blue Book, No. 365, *Myths of Religious Statistics*. Here I will say only that it showed a very marked decline of church-going between 1886 and 1903 -- the Church of England alone had lost 140,000 worshipers, although the population had very greatly increased -- that of 6,240,336 inhabitants of London only 1,252,433 went to church, and that there were less than 100,000 Roman Catholics in the six million people.

Most interesting of all was the division of the sexes: for the enumerators counted every man, woman, and child separately. I analyzed the figures, which are published in minute detail in the official report (*The Religious Life of London*, edited by R. Mudie Smith, 1904), in my *Religion of Woman* (1905). Omitting the Jews and taking the gross figures for Greater London (six million people), we have 372,264 men worshipers and 607,257 women worshipers. Most people are under the impression that the women outnumber the male worshipers by three or four to one. They are not even two to one. The above is an exact analysis of their proportions in a typical large city of an advanced modern civilization. And we must not forget that at the time women outnumbered men in the general population by about a million and a half. When we make allowance for that fact, we see that the greater religiosity of women merely means, at the outside, that three women go to church for every two men.

To get a little nearer to the truth we must examine this disproportion in different sects. There is no such thing as a typical religious psychology. The influences are quite different in different individuals, and we see this at once in these London figures. In the Church of Rome the women are more than twice as numerous as the men: in the Church of England less than twice as numerous: in the other churches much less than three to two. And where the local church is in a wealthy district -- where the men are generally college-educated and the services are more attractive esthetically -- the proportion of women worshipers reaches four to one. Taking four churches in the wealthier part of London, two Roman Catholic and two that call themselves English Catholic, the figures are:

- Brompton Oratory: 267 men and 1,105 women.
- Carmelite Church: 276 men and 807 women.
- Holy Trinity: 160 men and 880 women.
- Christ's Church: 249 men and 1,034 women.

The first of these was at the time the most ornate and wealthy Catholic church in England: the third was a ritualist Protestant church in the same wealthy district, and the Bishop of London was preaching there on the occasion of the census. In educated districts the Roman Catholic Church has habitually two to four times as many female worshipers as male.

The Nonconformist (Baptist, Wesleyan and Congregationalist) churches, on the other hand, have a disproportion of the sexes which is only slightly greater than their disproportion in the general population. In fact, we may say generally that Protestant or Evangelical churches in working class districts show (allowing for the larger number of females) little disproportion of the sexes. Here are the gross Protestant figures for three very large working class suburbs:

- East Ham: 4,996 men and 7,048 women.
- West Ham: 11,130 men and 16,230 women,
- Ilford: 4,585 men and 6,309 women.

In these districts, moreover, where the churches are not rich, where the music and "art" are poor and the men not well educated, even the Catholic women are not nearly twice as numerous in church as the men.

There is no reason whatever to think that London differs from American cities in this respect. In the large cities of what are called Catholic countries -- there are scarcely any such -- it is different. In Paris there are four women in church to one man. But in Protestant cities the proportion is likely to be about the same as in London. Susan B. Anthony once wrote that women form "from two-thirds to three-fourths of the membership of the Churches of America." She had no statistics to support that opinion, and we must be guided rather by the exact London statistics. Except where there is a special artistic attractiveness about the services, women-worshipers are not nearly twice as numerous as men-worshipers.

As the figures are loaded by this heavy disproportion of the sexes in ritualist places of worship, let us consider these first. It is quite a mistake to suppose that you explain it all by saying that woman is more emotional than man. Experimental psychology has shown, as I said, that she has not got a finer sensibility, a greater acuteness of sense-perception, than man, but it is clearly true that she is more emotional. Her functions and her sympathetic nervous system imply that. But there are several other things to be considered.

One is that priests make far greater efforts to secure female worshipers in wealthier than in poorer districts. The women are daintier and have ample leisure and more attractive homes. Visiting rich women is a delight to the priest: visiting poor women is -- I have, remember, lived in the clerical world -- a drudgery. Moreover, the visiting priest sees the women four times as much as he sees the men, and even the more pious women have their sense of his high sacerdotal character enhanced by sex-consciousness. The man is busy, he has lived in a skeptical atmosphere from college onward, he has no particular urge toward a priest of his own sex (he commonly distrusts him on account of his afternoon visits), and he has, as a rule, to leave his money to his family. The woman is the opposite in every respect. In other words, the fact that she is far more exposed to suggestion is the first thing to take into account.

Moreover, when we are explaining this heavy disproportion of the sexes in artistic ritualist churches, we have to consider another very important circumstance. Boys are nowadays rarely sent to sectarian schools, but girls are sent in very large numbers to be taught by nuns. From their teens onward the brother and sister are apt to come under quite different influences. The boy talks to other boys of every religion or none. The girl in a much higher proportion is expressly put in an environment which will promote and harden the habit of church-going. I do not mean that this great difference in the use of authority or suggestion explains the whole disproportion of sexes in ritualistic churches. The woman *is* more emotional than the man, and the express aim of these churches is to gratify her emotions. Yet, clearly, there are very many things to be taken into account besides her emotions. Priestcraft does not merely influence her more than it influences man. It is *used against her* far more than against the man. Considering that her education also is defective, she has far less chance of escaping. Already, as we are altering the college education of girls, we are rapidly lessening the disproportion of women in ritualistic churches.

These women, however, are a small minority. What concerns us more is the fact that generally, allowing for the fact that women far outnumber men, three women are religious to two men. What do we make of this? The exact figures I have given make the problem much smaller than most writers on the psychology of religion suppose it to be, and we need point only to a few influences or impulses to explain it.

That astute and fearless student of sex-matters, Mr. Havelock Ellis, has considered this situation (in his *Man and Woman*), but he started with the usual exaggerated idea of the religious disproportion of the sexes -- though he incidentally reminds us that of six hundred sects described in a dictionary of religions only seven were founded by women -- and I think this has colored his theory. He looks principally to the innate conservatism which the division of labor in family lite, especially in pre-civilized days, has given to woman. This and her greater emotionality and suggestibility, he thinks, explain the psychology of religion in this respect.

I distrust this theory of conservatism when I notice that the new sects (Theosophy, Christian Science, etc.) overwhelmingly attract women to their ranks. At all events, let us try first a less theoretical explanation.

We shall surely not be pushing an idea to extremes, but regarding the plain facts of life, if we say that the interest of the minister of religion makes him depend far more on the woman than on the man. He wants the children. From the fourth century onward it has been a tradition in the Christian Church that, if you have a mother or grown-up daughter zealous in a home, you have the best chance of securing the others. Priests will even (in broad language) urge wives to use their sex-attraction (by refusing or grudging it) in inducing a husband to go to church; and, in any case, hers is the chief influence on the children. It is, surely, an indisputable fact of life that she is exposed far more than the man is to priestly pressure.

Moreover, quite apart from wealth and education, the sex-instinct counts. The priest prefers women to men: women are drawn to priests far more than men are. Further differences arise from occupation and education. The man's business does not promote the frame of mind which church-going requires, while the monotonous work of the woman rather disposes her in favor of church-going. The man listens all his life to very free remarks about clergymen, religion, and sex, and such conversation rarely occurs in the presence of women. The man has had a more practical and realistic education, in school and in business, while the woman has much less occasion to develop the critical side of judgment. Quite a number of such contrasts could be enumerated.

In fine, there is strong confirmation of all this in the fact that, in proportion as we reduce the difference in education and environment between the sexes, we are reducing the disproportion of the sexes in religion. This generation is very apt to forget that the present comparative freedom of women Is a new thing. Two generations ago woman had, as a rule, from babyhood to old age, an entirely different experience from man. Now she gets the same education. She sports, smokes, drinks (since prohibition was adopted), swears, hears funny stories, has a club, works in an office, jazzes.... Ancient custom, lasting almost until this generation, explains more than psychology. It still lingers to a great extent. Many a man still regards the church mainly as an Insurance Society for the integrity of his property -- the faithfulness of his wife and chastity of his daughter -- and urges them to attend, while he goes to the club. It is a very complex question, yet simple in the sense that all the factors are very familiar matters. Woman goes to church far less than is generally supposed, and there is no need to seek mystic impulses in her nature to explain the slight disproportion of the sexes at worship.

Chapter III

Religion and Psycho-Analysis

This prosy analysis of the impulses at work in the mind and lite of a religious woman will give the reader some idea of my general attitude toward the subject of this Little Blue Book. If it seems, in comparison with some of the learned-looking essays you have read, superficial and materialistic, let me say that I learned it from the profound and spiritual authorities of my clerical years. "Things are not to be multiplied without necessity" is an axiom of Scholastic Theology: it means that, when you set out to explain a thing, you must try what known factors will explain before you drag in unknown. I want the reader to see for himself if, in his own sphere of observation, these many quite familiar agencies which I have enumerated do not suffice to explain the simple fact that there are three women worshipers to two male.

Thus since, like Professor Thouless, I find fanciful psychological explanations superfluous, I approach the Psycho-Analytic school on this subject in a critical mood. For reasons which cannot be discussed here the scientific world of our time suffers a perfect plague of new theories, most of which are the very truth for a few years and are then abandoned in out-of-date editions of encyclopedias. Indeed it is not merely the scientific world, but the general world of thought. Poets rage about new types of poetry, musicians about the "new music," sculptors about Rodin and Epstein, painters about Futurism and Cubism, and even economists and Socialists run on through a series of Marxian Socialism, Guild Socialism, Unionism, Direct Action, Credit Control, Anarchy, Soviet Socialism, etc., etc. It is not so much a new "psychology" in our generation as an expression of a new freedom and, particularly, a vast new literature, always itching for novelties, which broadcasts or megaphones every new idea and gives it a fictitious importance.

Having for thirty years observed philosophers, scientists, and economists hug their new theory for five or ten years and then discard it for another which was equally certain (and generally quite contradictory of the preceding), I have become in my mental attitude what I might describe as a conservative anarchist. I have no more respect for the authority of the hour than I have for the authority of Jesus Christ, Anthony Comstock, or the British or American Constitution....

Which means, in other words, that Psycho-Analysis may in the course of time shrink to the present size of Dergsonism, Futurism, Einsteinism, Mendelism, Modernism, Planetesimalism, etc. That, like most of these, it brings a permanent contribution to thought it seems safe to admit. But, quite apart from the commercial exploitation of it and the usual desperate applications of its principles to everything under the sun, it plainly has two of the familiar defects of new theories: it ignores or distorts many facts, and it has a great love of verbiage.

In its more familiar form, the Freud system, it seems to me, and now to most people, an extreme exaggeration of what is certainly a very large fact in life, sex; and when it is applied to religion it is quite untrue to experience. On this side there was a strong disposition on the part of thoughtful people to receive the Freudian explanation. As I have explained, the usual idea of the religiousness of women is very exaggerated, and the view was commonly taken that the repression of sex-feelings in unmarried girls and women was largely responsible. There is even now more sex-repression in young women than young men, though the situation is changing, but no one has ever clearly explained why the sort of poisoning or jaundicing of the psychic system by sex-repression should lead to greater religiousness.

I have read a new theory of something or other by a distinguished Psycho-Analyst which was, as he admitted, based upon "about a dozen" diagnoses. My own experience as a father-confessor (who is a kind of Psycho-Analyst) thirty years ago, in the course of which I heard thousands of confessions of young ladies, was that the bulk of them were no different in their attitude to religion than the men: that the really morbid amongst them were, though not married, by no means chaste; and that disorders of menstruation bad far more influence on them than suppressed sex-desire. At all events, the very plain influences I indicated in the last chapter do not leave much in the religious psychology of woman to be explained by sex, when we get the correct figures of disproportion of the sexes.

I have had the opportunity during recent years of making some study of the "psychology," in regard to religion, of young women between twenty and thirty. In few cases was there any serious religious feeling, though most of them belonged to one or other Church, and it seemed that, if anything, their sex-situation disposed them to rebel against religion. The clergy, as everybody knows, regard sexual feeling as the greatest cause of abandonment of religion; and I wonder if any would be so bold as to say that when young women in their twenties put an end to their sex-saturation by marriage they become less religious. It is, surely, rather the reverse. On the other hand, a very large acquaintance with Rationalist families convinces me that, when their daughters reach the stage of sex-development and repression they very rarely feel any new disposition toward religion. If they do begin to attend a church, as they sometimes do, the reason is confessedly social, recreational, or matrimonial.

Hence, while I have not space here to discuss the general truth of Freud's theory, I think that his application of it to religion is very theoretical, and it is certainly contrary to all my experience. That sex has nothing to do with the early evolution of religion itself I have explained in another volume, Little Blue Book No. 1008, *The Origin of Religion*. Religion is far older than phallic religion. Sex appears in connection with religion at a relatively high savage level, and what we call the religion of Melanesians, Australians, and still lower peoples is an attitude toward the spirits of the dead and the surrounding world in which there is not the slightest reason to suspect even a subconscious bias of sex. Its roots and causes are perfectly plain. It is entirely a matter of primitive reasoning on phenomena, tradition, and sentiments caused by these very definite and conscious beliefs.

It is said, in particular, that the very wide spread of a cult of a mother-goddess in old religions is due to the famous "Oedipus complex." Dr. E. Jones shortly defines this as "the impulse, gratified in primordial times, toward parricide and incest." Oedipus was the ancient Greek gentleman who, *quite ignorant that they were his parents,* having been reared in exile, slew his father and married his mother; and they were both so horrified when they learned their true relationship that Oedipus blinded himself, that he might never look his fellow mortals in the face again, and the mother killed herself. It is rather hard on the virtuous ancient Greeks that their Sunday School legend should be used to give a name to a supposed tendency of every male to hate his father and desire his mother. Oedipus never knew his parents. Moreover, it is a mere theory of certain fanciful sociologists (lightly adopted by H. G. Wells) that in "primordial times," the son, when he came to maturity, clubbed his father and mated with his mother. What about his sister, and the next man's daughter, who would be far more desirable? The facts even of lower savage life are entirely against the theory. As to ourselves and our Oedipus complex, I leave it to the reader, who knows just as much about it as Freud, to say if he thinks any large proportion of youths have an even subconscious desire of sexual intercourse with their mothers and are disposed on that account to hate their fathers. Life has a disconcerting way of being much less picturesque than our theories.

At all events, the mother-goddess has nothing to do with the Oedipus complex, because there is invariably a father god (generally the sky or sun) as well. The Cretan religion is the only one with a single female deity, and it is not primitive, but highly civilized. The mother-goddess is simply mother-earth fertilized by father-sky. It is a quite normal and healthy application to primitive religion (which existed long before this stage) of the ordinary sex-idea, not a taint from a subconscious poison.

Wherever this wonderful Oedipus complex, which seems to me totally false to the facts of life, is applied to religion, it is just as fantastical. One Psycho-Analyst writer uses it to explain Christ's love of his mother and indifference to his father. The facts are exactly the opposite. Taking the gospels for the moment as historical, but excluding *John*, which is notoriously a second-century romance, Jesus detested his mother, and was disliked by her, while his father seems to have died before the time described. Every word of Christ to or about his mother is harsh, and she joined his brothers in wanting to have the enthusiast put under restraint. He simply had the monastic (Essene) aversion from women.

In his *Essays in Applied Psychology* (1923) Dr. E. Jones tries several further applications of the new ideas to religion. The Oedipus practice of prehistoric men, we are told, is the root of the doctrine of original sin, and consequently of the Atonement. When the stage of morality was reached, men reacted with loathing upon the earlier practice of incest and called it the great sin or original sin. But the very few savage tribes which ever admitted incest with mothers -- we know hardly any -- are far below the level of ideas of original sin, and, when this legend appears, at the Babylonian and Egyptian level, there cannot possibly have been any knowledge of remote and obscure savages who practiced Oedipism. Moreover, the legend is as far removed from it as is the story of Jack the Giant-Killer.

Dr. Jones says that the characteristically Christian idea is surrender or subjection to the Father, not defiance of him. There, he says, you have the ethical reaction on Oedipism. Not in the least. The idea is not characteristically Christian, but is common to the whole group of pre-Christian religions with slain gods, and Frazer has plainly traced the whole evolution. The deity to be placated may be father or mother -- it is father in several religions besides Christianity -- but the primitive idea is that a god or representative of a god shall be slain lest he grow old and the fertility of the earth and men be reduced. (See Little Blue Book No. 1104., *The Myth of the Resurrection*.)

We are further told that the Holy Ghost was originally the mother goddess and was dislodged by reaction against Oedipism. The actual story of the evolution of the belief, which may be read in any history of dogma, is quite different. The Holy Ghost is an artificial creation out of words by the early Christian theologians, not a goddess turned male. The exclusion of Ishtar from Judea had nothing to do with a supposed Oedipus complex. It was due on the one hand to the Monotheism or monopoly imposed in their economic interest by the priests of Jahveh, and on the other to the ordinary Semitic contempt for women. Instead of showing any trace of an Oedipus complex, the Jews had a profound veneration for their fathers and precious little regard for their mothers.

In other words, the pressure of sex in the subconscious depths seems to have no more to do with the creation of specific religious beliefs than, as a rule, with the general religious attitude. In lands where there is no sex-repression in youth -- India, for instance -- people are far more religious than in a modern American city.

Colored girls, who are not much tainted with sex-repression, are scarcely less religious than white college-girls. In poorer districts and countries (Ireland, for instance), where marriage is early, the girls are far more religious than in late-marriage circles. A hundred sets of facts of real life are against the theory. Sex-starvation or perversion is apt to make young women unhealthy, and in a few cases this may have a religious expression. Facts do not justify us in saying more than that.

Psycho-Analysis of the Jung and Adler type, which keeps the sex-impulse in its place and speaks rather of a general surge upward from the subconscious of old vital impulses, throws no light on religion. There is no reason why suppressed impulses should find a religious expression. But the chief weakness of writers of both schools who discuss religion -- and I am not concerned otherwise with the theories -- is that they assume that there is something in the religious mood or attitude which has not yet been explained by more familiar and conscious impulses. We shall see that there is not. The roots of religion are in the conscious mind.

CHAPTER IV

The Religious Instinct

The next fallacy that we have to dismiss is the very common idea of writers on religion that there is a special urge or instinct or sense in the human breast which compels men and women to be religious. So frivolous are some of these serious and profound writers on religion that they only invented or discovered this religious instinct at a time when the general experience of the world entirely refuted it. No one heard of the religious instinct in the days when everybody was religious. It was invented when tens of millions of people in every advanced civilization abandoned all religion.

It was invented for the plain reason that the old type of argument for religion was being increasingly discredited. Deism shot to pieces the old arguments for Christianity in particular, which are based upon totally false historical statements. Then science and Agnosticism shattered the arguments for God and immortality. Apologists were reduced to the use of ancient "demonstrations" which had lost all intellectual respectability. Very well, they said, we will leave the material universe to science and the Bible to the Higher Critic. We will urge people to rely upon their own feelings about religion, and we will assure them that these are the pronouncements of a faculty, the religious sense, which is in its way as normal and authoritative as reason itself.

This idea grew out of the older psychology which is now entirely discarded. Instinct was supposed to be a "faculty" in the animal, and more feebly in man, just as reason, memory, will, etc., were "faculties." The word never meant more than a capability. If we can remember, desire, and reason, we obviously have, in a sense, the "faculties" to do these things. But the older philosophers and psychologists tended to take the abstract word in a more or less substantial sense. The "soul" was a spiritual substance, and its "faculties" were as real and distinct as the five senses. Today the soul and its faculties are regarded as relics of pre-scientific thought, and the idea that man has a special "faculty" for seeing religious truth has no meaning. The only real differences we can assign, are different regions of the brain for separate mental acts. Even Mrs. Besant has not ventured to find a brain-center for this religious faculty.

The word "instinct" was just as unfortunate. Half a century ago, when anthropology was imperfect, it was possible to hold that every branch of the human race believed in a God or gods. We have seen that this is quite false, but, while the belief lasted, the explanation of it was supposed to be that there was an instinct in human nature itself which impelled all men to believe in gods just as an instinct impelled all birds to mate and to build nests. The whole theory was miserably superficial even half a century ago. Since a crude reasoning power and a docility to tradition are actually common elements in all savages, the proper thing to do was to see if these would not explain the common religious beliefs. Savage belief is almost entirely a matter of blind acquiescence in tradition. Some writers -- Newman and others -- of the last generation even said that if children were brought up without either religious or anti-religious education, this "instinct" gave them religious sentiments and beliefs. You could test that today in the experience of millions of families. There is not a shred of truth in it.

Meantime science has made an end, not only of the supposed universality of belief in gods, but of the word instinct itself. We still, it is true, speak of an animal's habitual actions as instinctive, but we mean only that there is a certain structure or mechanism of nerve and muscle in an animal which acts automatically when it is stimulated. No matter how complex this mechanism may become by special evolution, it is always a mechanism. Of instinct as a "faculty" we know nothing.

The name is, therefore, altered, and we now generally read about a "religious sense." But the change of name is not of the slightest advantage to this antiquated and superficial theory. We know no "senses" except the special receptiveness or perceptiveness associated with differently constructed bodily organs, such as the eye and ear. Even what we call the internal sense is only a matter of the irritation of internal nerves. There is not the slightest analogy between what the physiologist or the psychologist calls our "senses" and what apologists call "the religious sense." You might just as well call it the religious diaphragm or selenium cell.

It is necessary to say this because religious writers blandly suppose that there are quite definite and recognizable meanings to their words when they talk about these things. There is no more definite meaning than there is in the mind of the pious but unphilosophical lady who says that God speaks "in her heart." And the more closely we examine what these writers mean, or can mean, the more clearly we see that this religious sense is manufactured, not as a theory to explain certain facts, but as a practical expedient to induce the faithful not to listen to skeptics. No psychologists will hear of it. Clerical writers alone are the "scientific" authorities for it. The idea of it is simply this: If you have a conviction that, let us say, there is a God, regard it as the authoritative declaration of some power in you which has as much right to a say in the matter as your reason.

But you have no right whatever to regard it as such if there is a plainer explanation of the presence of this conviction in you. In the long run the procedure is really humorous. A clergyman -- whether acting through the government in the school, or through parents in the home, or through clerical influence on the press, or directly in church -- plants in you from your earliest and most impressible days a conviction that there is a God. In children, obviously, such a conviction is a matter of authority. Most people remain children in that respect and never reflect on the ground of their conviction. Some may reflect on it, ask the reasons for belief, and consider them sound, but this "religious sense" is generally invoked in cases where there is some doubt about the soundness of the reasons. What it amounts to, therefore, is that the clergyman has implanted in you, directly or indirectly, a conviction that God exists, and he is now asking you to recognize this conviction itself as a proof of the existence of God! There is no other possible meaning in his appeal to your "inner voice" or "the whispers of your heart" or anything of that sort.

I once met a pompous ass of a believer who had this religious-sense theory in an exaggerated degree. It is not at all my custom to obtrude the question of religion in conversation, but somebody maliciously tried to draw the man into debate about God with me. He would say nothing but, with comic solemnity: "I *know* there is a God." He would not explain further, but his meaning was clear. He felt it. He sensed it. And there is but one possible form in which he could have given precise expression to his actual experience. He was visibly annoyed, but still silent, when I put it. It is: "I have a strong conviction that God exists."

A desperate apologist might say that, just as it is possible that such a man's conviction was due to education, it is also possible that it is due to a personal sense. You remember how Descartes, trying to bring his beliefs down to something which was absolutely certain, and might therefore be used as a safe foundation upon which to build, said: "I think, therefore I am." It is -- I should agree with Descartes anyway -- a plain declaration of the mind and is authoritative. Well, why may not some other voice or power or sense -- "Don't press me for exact definitions," this type of apologist implores -- say with equal authority within me: "God exists." The answer is simple. Things are not to be multiplied without necessity. You have a mind which is quite capable of saying to you, "God exists," and if you say that you have in addition this mystic voice, you must prove it. You can't. Your conviction may tell you a good deal about religion, but *it can tell you nothing about itself.*

In another volume (Little Blue Book No. 1060, *The Futility of Belief in God*) I have considered this religious sense or instinct from another point of view, and I gave there certain considerations which really dispense us from dealing further with it. The first is that it decreases as knowledge and intellectual development increase. The research which Professor Leuba (*The Belief in God and Immortality*), made into the proportion of believers and unbelievers amongst freshmen, sophomores, ordinary professors, and more distinguished professors affords very striking statistical evidence of this. As you rise in the scale of age and culture, the believers shrink from eighty to ten percent, the unbelievers grow from twenty to nearly ninety percent. Apart from this, it cannot be questioned that if you take five hundred farmers in Kentucky and compare them with five hundred university teachers, religious belief will be fairly solid amongst the farmers and absent from at least half the professors. It would be strange if a mental power grew feebler in proportion as we train and refine the mind. The real meaning is obvious. Religion is just an ordinary conviction in the mind and it is enfeebled when we accumulate knowledge, because it is essentially based upon ignorance. We see this on a very much broader scale in the collective experience of our time. There never was less religion in the world before, and there never was so much knowledge.

I further pointed out how this supposed religious sense gives entirely contradictory sentiments about religion, and even about God, in each different creed, sect, sub-sect, or phase of belief. The best educated religious believers of our time (Millikan, Lodge, Calkins, Adler, Pupin, etc.) are precisely the men different from each other as to the nature of God: and they all agree that the religious convictions of the crowd of pious believers are quite false. So belief has varied from age to age and country to country. Practically all educated men in China have had no religious sense whatever since the days of Kung-fu-tse and in Japan since Confucianism was introduced into that country. The thinkers of Greece, who meditated on religion as deeply as any body of men that ever existed, held every variety of opinion about it that can be conceived. Plato believed in a personal God and personal immortality: Aristotle believed in an impersonal and totally different God and denied immortality. The Pythagoreans and Eleatics believed that everything was spiritual: the Stoics held that even the gods, if there are any, are material: the Epicureans and Skeptics said that all religion was superstition. Roman thinkers and Moorish thinkers were just as divided, and the modern philosophic world is as far as ever from agreement.

In face of these masses of historical and contemporary facts it is futile to ask us to believe in a religious sense or instinct. Why should a million cultivated men like myself be totally devoid of it, and a million small store-keepers or Mexicans or Rumanian peasants have it in as robust a condition as their limbs? Why is it so constantly associated with stupidity and coarseness and so constantly dissociated from developed intellect and refinement? There is quite obviously no such thing as a special religious sense. We must take religious convictions and sentiments as we take any other beliefs and sentiments, and see if there is anything left which requires a special psychological explanation.

Chapter V

The Herd-Instinct and Religion

There is yet another theory of the psychology of religion that we must consider. There are, in fact, almost as many theories as there are religious thinkers, or thinkers about religion, but my readers will scarcely expect me here to discuss all the philosophic subtleties and novelties of Eucken, Bergson, Fouillée, Tagore, Royce, Croce, Seth, Ward, and every other modern religious thinker who invents some variation on the ancient theme and gathers a group of followers. If a single one of these gentlemen is correct, if a believer of any type is right, the essential truth for man, the real drama of life, in comparison with which the secular story of the race, is a puppet-show and the unfolding of the universe is a triviality, is the dialogue of the immortal soul and the eternal God. Yet it seems that there is nothing in the world so hard to discover as this. The theory refutes itself.

Let us turn rather to those more familiar aspects of our subject which are of general interest. You get here a further illustration of the evil to which I have drawn attention throughout these Little Blue Books. Even writers who regard themselves as profound are so really superficial that they very frequently do not even conceive exactly the subject they are discussing. Hundreds of writers of books and essays have in the last twenty years referred to or enlarged upon "the psychology of religion." It stands for something modern, profound, and precise. Well, what exactly do they mean by it?

Half these writers seem to mean the psychological conditions in which religion first appeared, and they speculate on these with a glorious indifference to the fact that the life of the lower savages today shows us how primitive man thought, felt, and reacted. When they do quote a few savages, they pay little or no attention to the cultural level of the people they quote; and they generally select a few instances which confirm their theory and ignore the rest. But I have devoted another volume (Little Blue Book No. 1008) to the origin of religion. It is a totally different question from the one we now confront. An idea or institution may arise for one reason and be maintained for quite a different reason.

I once noticed in a Queensland forest an interesting case of a parasite-tree. A wild fig grows parasitically up the trunk of a eucalypt, sucking its sap out of the eucalypt. After a time, the fig sends roots of its own into the soil, so that, by the time the eucalypt is sucked dry and killed, the fig is a sturdy tree living by its own roots and clasping in its arms the skeleton of the original eucalypt. I saw in this at once a figure of ecclesiastical Christianity growing upon the person and teachings of Jesus and then striking roots of its own in the soil of the Middle Ages. But it will serve as a figure of the growth of religion generally. Priestcraft, for instance, fastened upon religion parasitically when it became sappy enough to support a parasite and later struck its own roots in the soil.

But let us first attach a precise meaning to "the psychology of religion." It is a clumsy phrase. I use it only because it is familiar, but psychology is the whole science of mental behavior, not an interpretation of a particular thing. And what do we mean by "religion"? The objective body of doctrines, rituals, and priesthoods, or the subjective acceptance of them? I have, in any case, dealt in other Little Blue Books with the evolution of religion in the objective sense. We mean here religion as an attitude of belief and emotion. And again we have to ask, whose? There is almost nothing in common between the mental attitude of a liberal professor of theology at Chicago and of a peasant in southern Mexico, of a Theistic scientist and a Roman Catholic laundry woman or housemaid. All that we can do here is to take two broad classes, the ordinary and the intense or fanatical believer, with a few variations within each class, and analyze the mental attitude.

For the first class, the great mass of religious people throughout the world, there is a good deal of truth in the new theory to which I referred. Ten years ago a book entitled *Instincts of the Herd in Peace and War* (1916), by W. Trotter, was widely discussed. That period of intense collective emotion very naturally suggested a theory that human beings have a good deal of the herd-instinct which keeps together buffaloes or baboons and causes them to act in certain standard ways. Mr. Trotter, like all pioneers or discoverers of ideas, exaggerated, but in claiming that the herd-instinct is the principal cause of religious belief he had at least considerable facts in his favor. As I have already explained, I dislike the word instinct, but of the great mass of religious believers scattered over the earth it may justly be said that they believe and worship because the herd does.

Of eighteen hundred million worshipers far more than fifteen hundred millions -- say Chinese, Hindus, Latin Americans, the more backward races, and the mass of the peasantry everywhere -- e no "psychology of religion." They inherit religious beliefs as they inherit beliefs about cattle and babies. There is more "psychology," more variety of psychic elements, in their political than in their religious life. By the age of ten they are completely equipped with a set of religious beliefs, and for the rest of their lives their beliefs are based entirely upon authority, their practices follow almost automatically upon their beliefs or are guided by universal custom, and their emotions are not different in character from their political or domestic emotions. They have the same awe and reverence for God as for the king, and the great festivals of the year give them the same joy and excitement as secular rejoicings of political crises do.

There Is very little variation in this great body of worshipers beyond the variation of individual temperaments. Some are, notoriously, "more religious" than others: which means that they are more emotional generally or that they brood over the religious ideas more than the others do. You have just the same variations of emotional intensity in the political world, and it is therefore needless to ask for any special psychological explanation of the "piety" of many of these mass-believers. The Hindu is more fanatical about politics than about religion. Indeed, even in the domestic sphere you find analogous variations in wives and mothers, while in any body of, say, a thousand Democrats you will find the same variations in intensity of belief and emotion as in a body of a thousand Baptists.

Professor Thouless, whose book I have previously recommended because it avoids the meretricious practice of creating "a new and mystifying psychology for religion alone," identifies the psychological factors of the religious attitude as (1) the influence of tradition, (2) personal experience (consciousness of moral conflict and emotional life), and (3) processes of reasoning. There is another recent work, *Religion and the New Psychology* (1924), by a surgeon, N. B. Harman, but the title is rather misleading. It is a small collection of essays, and only the first deals with religion and psychology. The author, however, as far as he goes, is sound. The new psychology, he says, throws no special light on religion.

I agree entirely with Thouless, and I think that the reader will on reflection, merely adding that the consciousness of moral conflict seems to me only a rare and occasional ingredient in religion, and that these emotional experiences generally follow the religious attitude rather than help to engender it. In the religious life at least the emotions do not seem to any great extent to be influenced by the subconscious. They are provoked and sustained by definite conceptions of gods and goddesses, definite beliefs about life and the future, or by the images, ritual, music, hymns, etc., used in the cult. There is nothing specific in the emotions. They are the ordinary human emotions of joy, sorrow, hope, fear, reverence, love, etc., and, in proportion to the intensity or vividness with which the believer realizes or visualizes his beliefs, they arise as spontaneously as do the emotions of a young mother in regard to her first child.

Hence, although there is a very common practice of regarding this emotional life of the believer as his "religious life" in a special sense, you have only to consider it to see that it contains nothing specifically religious except the ideas or objects to which the emotions refer. It is only in the exceptional cases, which I study in the next chapter, that psychological analysis may discover points of special interest. A nun's love of Jesus, for instance, or a young monk's love of Mary may very well have a strong subconscious sexual coloring. In the overwhelming majority of believers the emotions are normal and have no specific religious or sexual meaning. What requires explanation, in other words, is the belief. Given the belief, the emotions follow as naturally as anger follows an injury, or gratitude follows a generous act, or hope and enthusiasm follow the acceptance of an economic creed.

And the factors of the belief are really only two in the mass of believers -- tradition and reasoning -- and in the case of the overwhelming majority only one, tradition. Parents, priests, and "the herd" make each new citizen of the world religious according to the pattern of the region in which he is born. I have in very ignorant parts of Europe, where everybody belonged to the Greek Church and most of the people never heard of any other, tried the effect of introducing the idea of skepticism. I do not mean that I tried to argue against religion, but merely to ascertain what would be the reaction of these people if I said that I was a skeptic and that half the people of my city were skeptics. The only effect was a dumb, almost pained, stupefaction. They were not really interested. It was a sort of outrage on their respect for tradition. They regarded me as a group of beavers or ants might regard an individual that by some freak did not follow the traditional ways. Such people -- and they are at least four-fifths of the religious believers of the world -- inherit their religion just as automatically as they inherit their code of etiquette or cooking or music. The authority of tradition explains entirely the fact that they believe -- the emotional religious life then follows of itself -- and back of tradition and its enforcement are the priesthoods.

Personal experiences count in the psychology of their religion only because they already believe. For ages man believed that the summer's crop, the rain supply, the fertility of the cattle, depended upon the gods, and this gave him a bias toward religion; but, obviously, the belief is the primary thing. Personal reasoning, on the other hand, has very little to do with religion in this largest class of worshipers. The world seems to them, in such dull gleams of reflection as they have, to be quite in harmony with their religion. The prosperity of the wicked and suffering of the good will be put right in the next world, and so on. Doubt never occurs to the overwhelming majority, and reason is not invoked to allay it. The stream of religious tradition flows placidly on.

The general truth of this, and the points at which variations begin to appear, can be seen best in America by studying the colored people. I have seen a body of colored worshipers in chapel, and have seen just the same frenzy at a political meeting for the abolition of the color-line and even in moving picture theaters, when Tom Mix or Duck Jones or Rin Tin Tin dashed upon the screen at the critical moment to save the heroine. I have listened for an hour to those chants or hymns which the colored folk of the south compose, and which give the finest expression of colored piety. The emotions are just the same as in courtship or politics. The objects of the emotions differ, and are provided solely by tradition, maintained chiefly in their own interest by preachers. And in the same colored population you see where the religion based solely on tradition passes into a religion based partly on personal experience. In the towns the colored folk hear skepticism, and the preachers buttress their faith for them with naive versions of the usual "Proofs." Once, at a colored meeting in Chicago, where my friend, Bishop Brown poured into his audience some scathing shots at orthodox Christianity, I noticed that large numbers even of the women shrieked with the same joy that they had once felt in chapel.

From that point, when the worshiper begins to reason, you get an increasing amount of personal element in the religion. Most people must know, however, that the great majority even of white believers in an educated country never reason, never need to reason, about religion. Today the "proofs" are provided with religion itself. The preacher adopts an apologetic tone occasionally, and slays Atheists, Modernists, Protestants, Catholics, or any type of opponent, and not one in five hundred of his audience will take the trouble to check his words. Reflect on the Fundamentalist's veneration for the Word of God. It is just a blind acceptance of tradition and priestly authority in ninety-nine cases out of a hundred.

In short, it is only a very small minority of religious worshipers whose religion offers any material for psychological study. In the overwhelming majority of cases a set of statements are planted in the young mind, and, as they are accepted by the whole community, they remain unchallenged. They are beliefs, or statements, accepted on authority. Where there is a variety of religions or sects, the diversity may provoke the believer to reflect, but as a rule his own sect has a literature so unblushingly mendacious that he never carries the inquiry beyond his own church. His religion as belief requires no analysis; and in so far as it is emotional, it has no special elements. Love of Jehovah, Jesus, Mohammed, Buddha, or the Bab is the same emotion as was once love of Ishtar or Tammuz or Zeus, and is now the love of friend or parent.

Chapter VI

The Psychology Of The Fanatic

In this analysis, or this claim that there is in religion nothing of a special nature to analyze, I am rigorously confining my attention to living men and women. It is the love of theory and of novelty that inspires most of these fanciful psychologies of religion. Let us stick to human facts. The difference between me now and what I was thirty-five years ago, when I was a devout believer, is not in the least psychological. I then, mainly on authority and partly for a time on personal conviction, accepted certain tremendous statements of fact: that an Infinite being read and was interested in my every thought, that I was presently going for eternity to a spiritual world, and so on. Naturally these statements and the dramatic ritual in which they were embodied, engendered very intense emotions in me. Scholars make a mistake when they take these emotions to be "religion." I have exactly the same emotions today, but they are not wasted on illusions. That is the only difference.

The only sense in which one can claim a psychological interest is by suggesting that, seeing that my friend of thirty-five years ago still worships in the same way, while I have now not an atom of religion, there may be some psychological element in him that is lacking in me. People say, in fact, that I have not "the religious temperament."

A little clear thinking will show any person that this is really the reverse of the truth. There is not some emotional element in my friend which I lack, but there is an intellectual element in me which he lacks. It is a question of the greater or less development of the critical quality, one might almost say, of suspicion. At the age of sixteen I began to press for "proof" of the large statements made to me by religion. Of ten companions (in a monastery) of about the same age not one felt the same critical urge, yet I was certainly the most emotional of them all. For ten years I felt that urge. Some of my companions in time felt the prick of it, but either suppressed it or affected to be easily satisfied. From the build of my mind I was unable to do either, and, from sheer intellectual urge, without any alteration of character or emotional temperament, I came to discard all religion. A "fanatic," as I really was, became logically one of the most irreligious of men.

Let us note in passing that many of the "fanatics" upon whom professors waste their psychological ingenuities have far less religion of an emotional sort than the professors believe. I have had opportunities of studying ministers of religion of various denominations who were regarded as men of great religious intensity, and their reputation was totally false. The day before I write this my eye falls on the name of a Catholic colleague thirty to forty years ago. He lives in his Church to an honored old age, much decorated with clerical dignities, esteemed all his life for piety. I knew him well. Whether he really believed the stuff or no I cannot tell, but he had far more hypocrisy than piety. Another priest-colleague I have known from boyhood as a most austere fanatic; and when I came to live in the same monastery with him I learned that he was a secret dipsomaniac, the scorn of his fellows. Another -- several others -- were vibrant with piety in the pulpit, and had mistresses in private. Bossuet, the famous Bishop of Meaux, who wrote works of classic piety, is now known to have had a secret wife or mistress. And the Catholic Church has no monopoly of this hypocrisy. I have found Protestant leaders and preachers of very unctuous exterior to have an extremely human scent for dollars and drinks. There is, in fact, no other caste of professional men that so often figures in the press in connection with women as ministers of religion; though most of their "scandals" are suppressed.

My point may be farther illustrated by a totally different set of facts. It is now extremely common to read that some man held his convictions with a "religious fervor," although this might refer to political, economic, humanitarian, or any other convictions. I have shown elsewhere that the leaders of the American Feminist movement, Mrs. Elizabeth Cady Stanton and Miss Susan B.

Anthony, were Agnostics, but it is always said that their cause was a religion to them. The majority of the most earnest idealists in the reform movements of Europe in the nineteenth century were Agnostics or Atheists.

In fact, the psychology of the idealist is so identical with that of the believer that he now often claims that his idealism is a "religion," and often (as in my own case) the word is thrust upon him in spite of his protests. In the Ethical Culture movement, for instance, and many of the Unitarian churches of America you have thousands of people claiming to be religious, yet totally rejecting the beliefs, in any shape, in God and immortality. You have professors constantly counting Confucianism, Stoicism, and Buddhism as religions, though Confucianism never had a God, Stoicism ignored gods and (clearly not believing in them) cut man quite away from them, and pure Buddhists are Agnostics. Yet the psychology of all these people on its emotional side is exactly the same as that of Theists and Christians.

In other words, there is no specific psychology, no religious psychology, at all. The emotions are the same in the fanatical or intense Prohibitionist, Puritan, Pacifist, Humanitarian, Agnostic, member of an Ethical Culture Society, and Christian. The same human heart responds in each case to an intensely felt stimulus. The readiness of modern writers to grant a "religious fervor" to all kinds of idealists shows that there is no religious fervor. Zealous people are sometimes zealous about religion, and sometimes about other matters. The zeal is the same.

Two or three small special classes alone call for any particular psychological treatment, but to build a "psychology of religion" on these very small groups is like building a psychology of human nature on a few hundred gunmen or drug-takers. One very select class is that studied by Professor W. James in his *Varieties of Religious Experience*. Realist as James generally was, he had in that work to cover such a vast world of biography that he has the facts wrong over and over again. He takes stories of famous "conversions" at their current value in religious literature and finds in them mystic factors which are totally unnecessary when one has the facts correctly. To take two of the most famous cases, I have shown in my *St. Augustine and His Age* that his conversion was a quite normal progress, innocently misrepresented by himself in later years, and in my *Candid History of the Jesuits* I have shown the same in regard to the "conversion" of St. Ignatius

Loyola. In all these cases there is no specific emotion, but a rare intensity of ordinary religious emotions; that is to say, ordinary emotions directed to religious ideas.

A second rare class are what is called "mystics." Writers on religion often forget that what the mystic, like the occultist, claims is a special intellectual, not emotional, outfit. A mystic is not a man or woman of exceptional ability, but a man or woman who claims to acquire religious knowledge by other than ordinary ways: by intuition, for instance. Their emotions are the same as those of other pietists. What is needed to explain their peculiarities is, not a psychology of religion, but a psychological explanation of a certain intellectual error or illusion. Advanced Theosophists, Spiritualist automatic writers, even certain meta physicians, have the same psychology. In large measure it is an indifference to the distinction between things imagined and things known, or a kind of affection for words whether or no they express realities. In many of these cases -- the St. Theresa, St. Clare, St. Catherine of Siena, etc. type-there is a legitimate field for the psycho-analyst. Their love of Jesus is largely suffused by subconscious sex-feeling, and in many cases they attached themselves to male saints in a very interesting manner. Such types, of smaller stature, are common in the Roman Catholic convent-world, but in the entire religious world they are an insignificant group.

A very different type is the girl who is really tainted by a kind of nerve-poison from sex-suppression. Religious abnormality is one of the forms in which this may find expression, but in my experience it is not very common. In the Catholic Church such girls often fasten upon the confessional as an outlet and simply gloat over their remorse for their sins. In some the condition easily lets them be persuaded that they may legitimately have sex-satisfaction with a minister of religion. In the Middle Ages it led to self-scourging and other fantastic tricks (even dancing) which became epidemic. Some sects (particularly Russian) have been known even in recent times in which an orgy of religious fervor ended in an orgy of sex-pleasure. All these abnormalities belong to very small minorities and cannot be treated in so small a work as this.

More widespread is the emotional craving which disposes many to dismiss the evidences for religion very leniently or even to dispense entirely with such. In another volume I told how so sane a thinker as Henry James believed in personal immortality because, he said, he wished to believe in it. More recently a well-known British Materialist, Robert Blatchford, became a Spiritualist, and told me that he did so at first entirely from emotional craving (for a belief that he would again see a dead wife). Spiritualism and Roman Catholicism no doubt make many converts, and bold large bodies of people, in this way. They wish to believe. They like to profess the beliefs or to share the ritualistic presentment of them.

The consciousness of sin or of moral struggle which some writers give as an important element of the psychology of religion seems to me an effect rather than a cause, or even an ingredient. There is no consciousness of "sin" until you believe in God. The "painful sense of moral struggle" is very largely a creation of moralists and spiritual writers. They create the feeling in a few people and then boast that religion meets it. Religion makes it far worse. The ordinary healthy man or woman is not conscious of legions of devils urging him or her to be unfaithful or to get drunk. One has to be firm sometimes, to decline an attraction, to refuse to lie or cheat, but one doesn't on that account groan and froth at the mouth. The "'moral struggle" is an accompaniment or effect of belief rather than an element of religion.

On the other hand, social and recreational considerations are world-wide factors in the "psychology of religion."' That is why, as I said in the first chapter, if the church and priest are not at hand, the religion soon disappears. In modern religion these considerations have a most important part. The church is a club. The minister caters to every interest, from dancing to matrimony, from vanity to sheer gregariousness and one's commercial interests. It pays a doctor to go to church, a lawyer to be a Catholic, a grocer to be religious, a professor to be on the side of the angels, a politician to rebuke infidelity.... The Almighty alone knows today how many of his worshipers believe in him. *He* could give us an entertaining volume on the psychology of religion.

www.ingramcontent.com/pod-product-compliance
Lightning Source LLC
Chambersburg PA
CBHW071752090426
42738CB00011B/2662